D0482458

A
gift
honoring
Griffin
and
Carson
Gilchrist

The Fan's Guide to
THE SPIDERWICK CHRONICLES

Also by Lois H. Gresh

THE FAN'S GUIDE TO
THE SPIDERWICK CHRONICLES

Unauthorized Fun with
Fairies, Ogres, Brownies, Boggarts,
and More!

LOIS H. GRESH

Illustrations by Greg Call

ST. MARTIN'S GRIFFIN
NEW YORK

ISBN-13: 978-0-312-35153-3
ISBN-10: 0-312-35153-4

First Edition: January 2008

10 9 8 7 6 5 4 3 2 1

To everyone who believes in magic!
And to Dan the Man, Flash Monkey!

Contents

Contents

The Fan's Guide to
THE SPIDERWICK CHRONICLES

✤ I ✤
So What's
It All About?

Dear Reader,

In November 2004, I was sitting in my editor's office, the very same editor who is publishing this book for you. His name is Marc, and he
lives in New York City. He told me that every
morning as he walks through the city on the way
to the publishing house where he works, he sees
flicks of light and color that come and go. I
asked Marc if he'd seen an eye doctor, and he
said, yes, he'd been to many eye experts, all of
whom told him that his eyes were perfectly fine.

So the next morning, I walked with Marc from his apartment to his office. I saw the same flicks of light and color.

But I also saw something more.

I saw tiny creatures flitting through the morning air, dancing on the breeze, alighting on the caps of the men who scurried toward their businesses and napping on the noses of fancy women who walked their long-haired Lapodazzickle dogs.

On a park bench, five tiny characters—and we're talking about characters who each stand perhaps one inch tall and weigh less than a hot dog—played lutes (which are sort of like guitars), fiddles (a country-western name for violins, in my opinion), and harps the size of your thumbnail. A man carrying two heavy suitcases sat on the park bench next to them. Well, naturally, I was horrified, thinking that the man was going to crush the five tiny musicians accidentally. As I gasped and bolted towards the bench to save them, the creatures danced into the air over the man's head. They settled on his bald spot and continued playing their music. I couldn't hear the songs, for they were probably as faint in sound as the band was small in size.

Marc was tugging at my sleeve. "Come on," he said, "I have to get to work. What's holding you up?" He didn't see the fairies.

For I knew that's what they were: fairies.

"These flicks of light, Marc, do you see them anywhere else?" I asked.

No, he told me, he only saw them while walking to work every morning.

A troop of fifty or more fairies scampered from a window onto a bunch of flowerpots. Several were dressed in Victorian garb, which means they were wearing ball gowns and velvet jackets from the late 1800s. Well, actually, the Victorian era was from about 1837 to 1901, when Queen Victoria ruled England. But that's beside the point. . . .

These Victorian fairies, along with countless others—some dressed in medieval outfits like torn leggings and tunics, others in astronaut's helmets and spacesuits (very curious, I thought), and still others in what looked like leaves and bark and nothing more—started digging through the earth in the flowerpots. As they extracted marbles, bits of paper, stones, keys, lint, wads of chewed gum, and half-eaten marshmallows, they jumped with joy and stuffed their new treasures into tiny sacks.

Marc stood with me on the sun-dappled sidewalk. He gazed at the flicks of light. I marveled at the fairies.

"Lois, what's it all about?" he said.

I turned from the tiny treasure seekers and blinked at my editor. "It's about magic. It's about a world we know nothing about, Marc. But it's there, all around us."

And so, my dear reader, what *is* it all about?

Check out *The Spiderwick Chronicles* by Tony DiTerlizzi and Holly Black.[1] Tony and Holly know all
about fairies, and if you've read their books,
then you know all about fairies, too.

This book, the very one you hold in your
hands, is all about *The Spiderwick Chronicles*: the
characters, the creatures, the places. It has hip,
cool, fun facts about the *Spiderwick* world that you
won't find collected anywhere else. It has games,
anecdotes (also known as "little stories that allow
the author to ramble incoherently for ten minutes"), and little-known references about goblins, griffins, fairies, dwarves, dragons, elves,
ogres, unicorns, trolls, and other magical fan-
tasy creatures. I hope it's as much fun for you to
read as it was for me to write.

—*Lois Gresh*

---

[1] A series of five books published by Simon and Schuster Books for
Young Readers, New York, 2003–2004.

So let's begin . . .

What *is* it all about, this world of *The Spiderwick Chronicles*?

The first book is *The Spiderwick Chronicles: The Field Guide (Book One of Five)*, and it was published in 2003 by Simon and Schuster Books for Young Readers in New York City. In this first book Jared Grace, his identical twin Simon, and their sister Mallory, go to live in their elderly Aunt Lucinda's dilapidated (which means "ramshackle"—which doesn't have anything to do with rams but rather means "broken down and in great need of repair") carriage house. From the description in the book, this house looks really creepy. If I had to live in a house like that, I would have nightmares.

Jared and Simon are in fourth grade. Their sister is a little older and likes to fence with swords. This is a very unusual hobby for a fourth grader, and it comes in handy later in the Spiderwick books. Now, I have an older brother, and while he never spent Saturdays swordfighting in our backyard, he did have a plastic blow-up punching bag in our basement. He was extremely skinny, so he looked pretty silly punching a plastic blow-up bear, and I don't think the effort of punching the plastic bear built up his muscles at all. As for me, my hobbies were chasing frogs, riding my bike, and walking on the tops of fences. I would have been afraid to swordfight when I was Mallory's age.

But let's return to rams for a moment. When the three kids arrive with their mother at Aunt Lucinda's ramshackle house, they immediately learn a few things: first, that the door knocker is in the shape of a ram's head (and now we can dispense with rams for the rest of this book); second, that despite the fact that it's as large as twelve shacks, the house indeed looks like a pile of shacks; and third and perhaps most important, that the house is weird and mysterious.

Does your apartment or house have a knocker on the front door? My house does not have a door-knocker. If it had a ram's head knocker, I'd certainly wonder why, and in fact, I'm still wondering why Aunt Lucinda's house has a ram's head door-knocker.

In the ram's head house, something seems to be living in the kitchen walls. Whatever this thing is, it's tiny, it collects bits of debris, and it also causes a lot of trouble.

If you live in the city, perhaps mice live in your kitchen walls. If you live in the country, you might have a squirrel in there, but it's unlikely. Though my neighbor tells me that he regularly rounds up gigantic, fifty-pound raccoons in his yard, so if I ever hear a racket in my kitchen walls, it might be due to a pack of fat raccoons.

While Jared, Simon, and Mallory try to figure out what's in the walls, not thinking for a second that they might have raccoons, Jared must cope with the fact that he's been getting in trouble and failing in school ever since his father left the family. Jared's mother, used to her son getting in trouble by now, immediately blames him whenever something goes wrong. This is very depressing for Jared. Sure, he's miserable because his father left them and now they're poor and his mother works all the time and, well, he just misses having his whole family together; but still, he doesn't want to get in trouble all the time and flunk out of school. So Jared is sad and confused.

I expect that most kids would be sad and confused if they were in Jared's shoes. It's tough when you're in a family with only one parent and there's not enough money to pay the bills. It's no fun to leave your friends and move far away to a place that reminds you of a haunted house. And it's not as if people are understanding, so if your grades start to slip, people just look at you as if you're always going to be a failure. It's hard to get them to change their opinion about you. So it makes sense that Jared is sad and confused, doesn't it?

At night, Mallory hears the creatures in her bedroom walls. With the loudest noises coming from the kitchen, the three kids sneak downstairs in the middle of the night to investigate. They find a dumbwaiter, an old device used to send things from the kitchen to other floors in the house. Jared climbs in, armed with a bit of candle, and he ends up in a secret library room, where all the books are about weird things like fairies.

When I was Jared's age, I would have climbed into a dumbwaiter in the kitchen wall, too. I doubt that I would have done it with a bit of candle, though. I might have used a flashlight, but then, I had one of those and I didn't own any candles. Nor did I know where my mother kept matches. Plus, she would have killed me if I played with matches and candles!

When Mallory wakes up the next morning, her hair is tied to the bedposts, and it takes their mother forever to unknot her. Of course, Jared is blamed, despite the fact that he had absolutely nothing to do with it. Depressed, Jared returns to the secret library room, where he finds a note waiting for him. The note tells him to look for a man's torso, and Jared figures out that the riddle means that he should look in a nearby "treasure" chest. The chest belonged to someone named Arthur Spiderwick.

Right away, we (the readers) know that Jared is actually smart. His teachers may throw him out of school, but here he figures out a difficult riddle to find a treasure chest.

In the chest, Jared finds The Field Guide about fairies.

I should note that, although I'm a grown-up

woman, I love Tony DiTerlizzi's illustrations throughout the five *Spiderwick* books. For example, look at the drawing of Jared on page 35 of Book One. How can you help but like Jared after seeing this picture of him? And how about the drawing of Mallory with her hair tied to the bed on page 42? That's just too funny!

Well, while Jared is learning about fairies in the secret library room, Mallory is fencing with Simon in the yard. Specifically, Mallory has Simon up against the ruins of a carriage house, and his thrusts and parries are becoming weaker and weaker. A long time ago, I was playing catch with my older brother, and I tossed the ball to him. It hit his mouth (by accident, I swear!) and broke a tooth. My father was furious and spanked me much too hard, and my mother held the "tooth incident" against me for years. In fact, she finally stopped bringing it up maybe five years ago, and I'm pretty old by now. This "tooth incident" followed me around forever.

Had I forced him against a fence using a sword, I would have been thrown out of the family and sent to an orphanage or foster home. Mallory's lucky that her mother never pays attention to what she's doing with those swords.

Anyway, when Simon is under attack he uses a parry, which deflects (meaning "pushes away") Mallory's sword. He doesn't seem to have the skills to make a riposte, which is a quick return thrust.

My guess is that Mallory uses a foil, one of the three main types of swords used by fencers. The other two types are the épée and the saber. A foil has a flexible blade and weighs about one pound. The épée is about the same length as the foil—thirty-five inches—but the épée weighs about twenty-seven ounces, meaning it's almost twice as heavy as the foil. The épée is actually the modern version of the dueling swords used long ago. Remember when men in movies and books would duel each other with swords over a woman, some land, or just their honor? They were using old-fashioned épée swords. The épée has a much stiffer blade than the foil and is probably more dangerous and less likely to be used by a young girl.

And then there's the saber. Mallory definitely is not using a saber with her brother, Simon. Sabers were used by cavalries, or armies, long ago. The blade isn't at all blunt; rather, it *cuts.* This is a very nasty weapon.

With Aunt Lucinda living in an institution and their mother often gone either to work or the grocery store (her life sounds a lot like mine), Jared, Simon, and Mallory explore the house, read The Field Guide, and look for the creatures who dwell in the walls. Jared thinks the creatures might be brownies, pixies, or boggarts (see chapter 5 for the lowdown about brownies, pixies, boggarts, and all sorts of other magical creatures).

Now what do you think The Field Guide suggests you do if you want to find a brownie or boggart in your house? Do you play harp music? Do you excel at basketball because maybe, just maybe, boggarts are All-Star Hoopsters? Do you bake ten trays of brownies and leave them all on the counters so the brownie feels right at home? Do you tap dance at midnight? Personally, I'd try the ten trays of brownies and the tap dancing, but that's not what The Field Guide says to do.

The Field Guide suggests that a person sprinkle flour or sugar all over the floor to capture the footprints of the brownie or boggart living in the house. That's pretty clever, I think. And if you're wondering what a boggart *is*, according to the Field Guide, it's a brownie gone bad.

Rather than tap dance, Jared does as the book instructs: he scatters flour on the kitchen floor. He also puts out a saucer of milk, hoping to attract his brownie/boggart. Maybe he thinks boggarts are like cats and can't resist saucers of milk. Or maybe he thinks boggarts like Froot Loops cereal, and the milk will attract them to the kitchen to find the cereal in the pantry. Or maybe he's just doing what The Field Guide tells him to do, which could be the case, given that I made up all that stuff about boggarts being like cats or liking Froot Loops cereal. At any rate, as you might guess, his mother catches him and sends him back to bed.

Of course, by the next morning, the brownie/boggart has destroyed the kitchen, and poor Jared gets in trouble yet again. But the footprints are there, so clearly there's some magical little guy running around the house.

My kitchen usually looks a mess when I get up in the morning. It's never occurred to me that a boggart might be causing me all this trouble. I've always assumed it was my son Dan, who eats huge amounts of pizza every night. Is it possible that someone else is in the house with us, someone with a huge appetite for pizza and a huge habit of littering the counters with pizza crusts and sauce?

We don't have a dumbwaiter here, so there's no way for me to ride up and down holding a candle stub and seeking a secret room in the house. But there is an old chimney. I wonder if I can crawl around in there, looking for the entrance to a secret room of fairy wonders.

Let me think further about all this. . . .

We do live in an ancient Victorian house, though ours is small compared to the one in which Jared lives with his brother, sister, and mother. But our walls are thick, so they may indeed contain hidden rooms.

The more I think about it, the more convinced I am that Dan and I have a boggart living in the house with us. It all makes perfect sense. After all, Dan is tall and thin, yet the kitchen is destroyed every morning with food debris, so it's logical to conclude that a boggart is eating all the food and leaving crusts and sauce everywhere.

At any rate, Jared finally takes Simon to the secret room, where the two boys encounter the boggart for the first time. His name is Thimbletack, and he's tiny. He talks in riddles.

As *The Spiderwick Chronicles: The Seeing Stone (Book Two of Five* opens, Jared gets in trouble at school for drawing pictures of brownies and boggarts in class instead of paying attention. Angry, he rips a kid's notebook in half and then falls into a funk, remembering his parents' divorce and how happy life was when they were all a family.

Are your parents divorced? If not, you're lucky, and I hope that your family is really happy. But if they are, don't let it get you down so much that you rip up kids' notebooks. Our family is broken, too, and after it happened, Dan infested his school with fruit flies—by accident, but still. . . .

We've never really gotten used to the fact that Dan's father is gone, but we've muddled along and been pretty happy, anyway. It helps to play Crazy Zombie, to play lots of games of Zombie Fast-Food Restaurant, and to play with zombie action figures. I'm seeing a theme here. It has something to do with zombies. I actually know how real-life zombies are created, because I wrote about that subject in another book,[2] but I won't bore you with the horrifying details here.

Simon ends up disappearing in *The Seeing Stone*, and Jared must use a funny eyepiece to see all the creatures in the fairy world as he tries to find his twin brother. The eyepiece enables Jared to see a pack of five goblins in the yard. As the goblins attack Jared, Mallory uses her rapier (a fancy word for sword) to beat back the goblins and save her brother.

---

[2] Lois H. Gresh, *The Truth Behind A Series of Unfortunate Events: Eyeballs, Leeches, Hypnotism, and Orphans—Exploring Lemony Snicket's World* (New York: St. Martin's Press 2004).

Continuing the search for Simon, Jared and Mallory end up in the woods, where they fight their way through jewelweed and vines.

Jewelweed are actually beautiful flowers that look like impatiens, which are commonly grown in summer gardens. Some forms of jewelweed, however, can be as tall as five feet and look like bushes. The spotted jewelweed, for example, grows in dense clusters with many five-foot-tall bushes packed tightly together. It would be hard to make it through a forest filled with vines and jewelweed, but this is what Jared and Mallory do.

Eventually, they reach an oak tree with sprites on the branches. The sprites are tiny fairies. But then something frightening happens: a giant ogre rises from a stream where Mallory has fallen!

After running away from the ogre, Jared and Mallory reach a goblin camp, where the goblins are gnawing on bones, and they see animals of all kinds in cages lined with what appears to be poison ivy. Inside one of the cages is Simon.

The goblins have also captured a griffin, which is a gigantic magical bird. Along with rescuing Simon, Jared, and Mallory end up rescuing the griffin. Because Hogsqueal, a goblin in a cage, gives them a magic rag that enables them to see fairies without using the eyepiece, the kids save Hogsqueal, too.

After another adventure, this time with a ten-foot-tall troll, everyone—Jared, Mallory, Simon, Hogsqueal, and the griffin—heads home.

As *The Spiderwick Chronicles: Lucinda's Secret (Book Three of Five)* opens, we learn that Hogsqueal is a hobgoblin rather than an ordinary goblin, though we're not sure how the two differ. For my attempt to explain the difference, see chapter 5.

So what does the griffin eat while he's staying in the dilapidated carriage house? Chickpeas and watermelon? Ice cream and cantaloupe? Fried chicken with mashed potatoes? Linguini vongole with clam sauce? Hamburger ground up with corn flakes? *Bingo*. I knew we'd hit upon the right answer eventually, and it happens to be hamburger ground up with corn flakes. A lot of it.

What would you do if you had Thimbletack wrecking your house and getting you in trouble with your mom? Jared eventually comes up with a solution—a pretty remarkable and kind solution, I think—but it takes awhile to figure out what to do. To get advice, the kids go to the institution where their Aunt Lucinda lives. With her are more sprites, who offer Simon magical fairy fruits, which apparently are very dangerous.

With Thimbletack in control of The Field Guide, Jared, Mallory, and Simon return to the secret library room in their house to seek clues. They find a map marked with words such as *trolls, dwarves,* and *sprites.* They begin to wonder where Arthur Spiderwick went, and if he went there against his will.

Off they go, hoping to find Arthur Spiderwick. Along the way they encounter a phooka, another shape-shifter, which means he can turn into a monkey, a snake, a bird, or a blob anytime he wants.

Now, if you could shape-shift into any form, what form would you choose? Remember, you could be anything you want. An airplane, a teacher, an elephant, or a tiger—anything. It might be fun to shape-shift into a dog or cat, just for a short while. Then you could run around outside like your pet (if you have one) and see what life is like for a bird-chasing, chow-eating, furry beast. I suppose that you'd still be able to talk and think in your human language (for example, English rather than Barking). Only your *shape* would change. Your mind would remain the same, and you'd still be able to read books, watch television, talk on the phone, and so forth.

After meeting the shape-shifting phooka, Jared, Simon, and Mallory meet three elves, who demand that the kids give The Field Guide to them. They say that humans destroy the forests and kill all the creatures who live in forests. Few fairies and other magical creatures are left, and those who remain must be protected from people. With The Field Guide, people can find the fairies and kill more of them.

What's interesting to me is that humans will destroy the forests whether they have The Field Guide or not. In reality, there's no Field Guide, and companies and governments destroy forests all the time. If I were a fairy, I really wouldn't want people to know how to find me. I'd be terrified that greedy people would find me, capture me for the zoo, cage me, torture me, kill me— something terrible—and I would want to hide, too. Imagine if a big corporation got hold of a fairy with her fairy fruits. Greed would instantly overcome any human desire to be kind to the fairy. So I can easily understand why the elves demand that the kids turn over The Field Guide.

Eventually, we shift into *The Spiderwick Chronicles: The Ironwood Tree (Book Four of Five)*, where many strange things happen and the whole story is tied up into one neat ending. I assume that you have read the entire *Spiderwick* series of books (if you haven't read them yet, you should rush out right now and get them). But just in case you haven't read the last book yet (and if not, well, why haven't you read it yet?), I don't want to give away the ending or any of the surprises.

Jared does get into trouble again, and his mother calls his estranged father, who left them for a new life somewhere else, and tells the father that Jared is "really out of hand" and she "can't take care of him"—and that maybe it's time for Jared to live elsewhere.

Clearly, this isn't something any kid wants to overhear, and it only makes Jared more determined to prove his innocence in this whole evil-fairy business and make his mother see the truth: that he is a good kid, that he isn't causing all the trouble at all. It's not Jared's fault, after all, that fairies are shape-shifting into people who look exactly like Simon and him.

By the time we finish reading the last book, everything has calmed down.

And now, you're going to hate me for telling you this, but . . .

We end each chapter of this book with a Fast Fact Quiz. All the quizzes are secret standardized tests developed by the National Teachers Union to determine your IQ. If you flunk the quizzes in this book, the union will demote you to nursery school, where you'll be forced to play Foxy Woxy in Chicken Little plays for the rest of your life. So be really careful and use a number two pencil. Mark your answers clearly and then double-check them.

✦ So What's It All About? ✦

Okay, I bet you're scared half out of your wits by the thought of these hard quizzes. Calm down, be cool. I swear: these quizzes are a piece of cake! Here's an example:

Fast Fact Quiz!

Which character uses a light saber to cut brownies in the kitchen?

⭕ Answer 1: Mallory, who has the Force and prefers to duel extra dark chocolate brownies with walnuts.

⭕ Answer 2: Simon, who parries the brownies into crumbs before eating them.

⭕ Answer 3: Jared, who follows the instructions in The Field Guide to cut and eat brownies.

⭕ Answer 4: None of the above—but Mallory could have been a Jedi in some past life.

Easy, huh? Oh, whoops, wait a minute. That's not one of the quiz questions. It could be, and the real answer is #4, but such a quiz question would flunk you straight back to nursery school for sure. We wouldn't do that to you, but we might ask your opinion about some of the characters. For example:

Fast Fact Quiz

Who do you think is the most similar to Jared?

◯ Answer 1: A brownie or boggart named Thimbletack, who is actually not such a bad guy; he's just misunderstood, just like Jared is misunderstood.

◯ Answer 2: A vixen, pixie, cupcake man, or dragon.

◯ Answer 3: An ogre with the breath of an elderly ox.

◯ Answer 4: A raccoon.

The correct answer is #1. See? You just learned something about the boggart. Sure, his name is revealed in *The Seeing Stone,* so that's nothing new. But did you ever notice how similar Thimbletack is to poor Jared? Both of them get in trouble all the time, yet both are just lonely and kind of depressed. They don't really mean any harm. So you just learned something new by taking a very tricky test, and it makes sense for us to report your amazing accomplishment to the National Teachers Union. You can't lose with this book!

In fact, if you don't know the answers to the Fast Fact Quizzes, we even give you a cheat sheet—see Appendix B on page 147.

Of course, you can't trust me about the answers. For example, I told you that Thimbletack is just a misunderstood brownie who isn't really a mean and nasty boggart at all. But that's not entirely true. I believe in the deepest recesses of my heart—as opposed to the shallowest recesses of my liver—that Thimbletack is naughty. Otherwise, why would he tie Mallory's hair to the bedposts? It was so bad that her mother had to chop off all her hair to free her. I may be a misunderstood wretch myself, but that doesn't mean I tie my boss's hair to his computer monitor (not that he has that much hair) and force his mother to come from halfway across the world (where he grew up) to untie him. I would get fired. As an adult, I wouldn't be called naughty. Instead, I'd be called something much worse, like insane. And I wouldn't like that. So even as a misunderstood wretch, I don't tie people's hair to fences, cars, refrigerators, bedposts, or computer monitors. I think Thimbletack is a *Bad Boy*.

But I do like him. He's funny.

Here's your real Fast Fact Quiz, the one with the answer in Appendix B.

Fast Fact Quiz!

Marc is:

○ Answer 1: a goblin who sends Jared, Simon, and Mallory into the clutches of the griffin.

○ Answer 2: a goblin who falls in love with a griffin, only to learn that the griffin is really a troll.

○ Answer 3: the editor of this book.

○ Answer 4: a goblin who becomes a master cat chef on early morning television shows.

✦ 2 ✦

Are You A
Spiderwick Fanatic?

Are you a *Spiderwick* fanatic?

The answer is yes if:

- you tell your teacher that an ogre ate your homework.
- you make wind chimes out of soda cans and have campouts with your goblins . . . er, friends.
- you blame your bad grades on trolls.
- you keep researching the locations of all the gravel pits within a 500-mile radius of your house, hoping to find one with fairies.

- you refuse to eat meatloaf for dinner, telling your mother that you'll only eat fairy fruits from now on.
- when the principal calls you into his office, you pull out a fencing foil and say, "*En garde, my man!*"
- when a neighbor tells your mother that you broke the neighbor's basement window, you blame it on the "non" you (for example, if your name is Archibald, you would blame "non-Archibald").
- you insist that your parents move from their city apartment to a dump on the outskirts of town that looks like twelve shacks piled on top of each other.
- you insist that your mother install a rusty ram's-head knocker on the front door.
- you drag giant birds home on a tarp.
- you tie your waist-long hair to the bed using ultratight knots, then blame it all on hobgoblins.

- every night after your mother goes to bed, you put ten trays of brownies on the kitchen counter, hoping to attract household brownies and boggarts.

- you walk around school with a piece of glass clipped to your nose and tell your friends that sprites are dancing on their desks.

- you call the school bully "Lord Korting."

- you insist that your name is Hogsqueal and you don't answer to your real name anymore. Teachers would be forced to call on you in class by saying things like, "Hogsqueal, in what year was the Declaration of Independence signed?"

Fast Fact Quiz!

A boggart is:

○ Answer 1: a young guy who brags too much and slicks back his hair with grease.

○ Answer 2: an old guy who starred in a lot of films in the 1940s.

○ Answer 3: a naughty brownie.

○ Answer 4: a naughty chocolate chip cookie.

A Story About the Fairy Morgan le Fay

Have you ever heard of King Arthur and his Knights of the Round Table? It's a legendary story that includes famous characters such as Merlin, Sir Lancelot, and Guinevere. King Arthur himself was a great figure, representing the might of good over evil, the power of light over darkness, and the eternal struggle between right and wrong.

In the Arthurian tales, Morgan le Fay is the daughter of Arthur's mother, Igraine, and her first husband, the Duke of Cornwall. This means that Morgan le Fay is Arthur's half sister.

You'd think his own half sister might help him, especially when you consider what a great guy Arthur is, but alas, Morgan le Fay operates largely as Arthur's adversary. She gives the Excalibur sword to Accolon, her boyfriend, so he can wield the mighty power of the sword (as powerful as a Jedi's light saber) against Arthur. She goes so far as to steal the scabbard of Excalibur, which can protect Arthur, and she throws the scabbard into a lake.

But the legend also shows Morgan le Fay as being kind to Arthur. For example, she takes Arthur to the fairy island of Avalon so he can be healed. Morgan le Fay often has been portrayed as a healer and shape-shifter who grew up on Avalon, which is also known as the Isle of Apples. In fact, Morgan tells Arthur she can heal him only if he stays with her for a very long time.

Many people believe that Morgan le Fay is a

fairy. They point to her role as an enchantress of King Arthur, that she might have learned the Old Ways while growing up on Avalon, which, after all, *is* a fairy island. They point out that Morgan was a fairy queen, a ruler of Avalon, and somewhat of a priestess while growing up. They point out that while Christianity was supplanting pagan ways in Britain, Morgan le Fay remained true to the fairy faith. Why would she defend fairyhood so much if she wasn't a fairy herself?

One thing is sure: Morgan le Fay seems to possess magical powers and can cast spells that alter the appearance of reality.

Known as Fata Morgana, Morgaine, Morgue la Faye, and other names, she is also believed to be the Lady of the Lake, a true healing spirit who takes the wounded King Arthur to Avalon. Many scholars say that Morgan le Fay's magic is directly responsible for the fake images, or mirages, in the Straits of Messina that lie between

Italy and Sicily. These scholars say the sorceress Morgan le Fay likes to create magical cities that float on the clouds. And in the Straits of Messina, people routinely see mirages of a city suspended in midair. They see not just the buildings but people like themselves scurrying around the city. Such a mirage is called a *fata morgana,* after its creator.

Of course, science can explain away the magical images by telling us that the mirages are created when light bends between layers of warm and cold Mediterranean air. Because the weather is stable in the Straits of Messina, there are many layers of air, and they reflect the images of the coastal towns.

Science can explain anything. But so can fairy magic.

✦ 3 ✦
Spiderwick Characters:
Good Guys vs. Scum and Filth

It's always about Scum and Filth, isn't it? All the best stories are about good guys battling the most vile Scum and Filth in the universe. We expect the good guys to win, and we have faith that they'll always come out on top. But somehow, we always worry that they'll get really hurt, that maybe they won't wobble to their feet using their last shred of strength and then beat off those bad guys and save the world, their mother, their home, their own dignity.

It's exciting, and we can't get enough of it.

How good a story is depends on how good the heroes are and how bad the Scum and Filth turn out to be. Are they evenly matched? Or better yet, are the bad guys a little stronger than the good guys, posing a horrible threat to people everywhere?

The Spiderwick Chronicles feature three main good guys: Jared, our hero; Simon, his twin brother; and Mallory, his sister. Other good guys include minor characters such as their mother and Aunt Lucinda, but most of the action takes place with Jared, Simon, and Mallory. There are a few other good guys, of course, such as the griffin and Thimbletack (he's good sometimes and naughty at other times).

Because he's the main hero, we'll talk about Jared first. He's always trying to do the right thing, isn't he? Yet Jared keeps getting in trouble. In fact, it gets so bad that Jared's mother is thinking of dumping him on his father because she thinks he's too "out of hand" and she can't take care of him anymore.

But we know, as we're reading these books, that Jared is the real hero. He's the one who climbs into the dumbwaiter and finds the secret room. He's the one who always decodes The Field Guide, who figures out how to see fairies with the weird little nose-clipped eyepiece. He's the one who is determined to find what's living in the house walls, even if it means that his mother's going to get really mad at him for a long time. Jared saves Mallory and Simon by outsmarting the troll; he points out that goblins are juicy and fat, diverting the troll's attention from the children to the goblins.

It's Jared's obstinacy (this means that he's very stubborn) that, in the end, saves the day. After all, what would have happened if Jared hadn't bothered to find out what was in the house walls? Would the boggart had driven his family into the streets to live?

Simon, who is Jared's twin brother, serves a few important roles, however. For instance, he protects Byron the griffin from certain death at the hands of the goblins. Then he makes sure the kids get the tarp from their home, return, and drag Byron back to the carriage house. Simon also helps Jared and believes in his brother's goodness and honesty.

Mallory also stands by Jared when their mother blames Jared for all sorts of calamities (which means "disasters"). Her fencing skills come in very handy throughout the five-book series. She's courageous and loyal.

As for bad guys, well, take your pick! You can choose from monsters, ogres, hundreds of goblins, dwarves, or the troll. These characters aren't like people in *The Spiderwick Chronicles.* That is, they don't have personalities. They aren't portrayed as individuals. They're just BAD GUYS. Every goblin eats cats, for example, and every goblin is going to cause trouble without thinking twice about it.

There are so many bad guys in these books that as soon as Jared, Simon, and Mallory outwit one kind, several other types pop up to cause them trouble. They escape from dwarves, only to be chased by hordes of mechanical robot dogs. They escape from goblins, only to encounter Lord Mulgarath. They escape from Mulgarath, only to run into dragons. And so forth. You can read all about these bad guys in chapter 5.

Fast Fact Quiz!

An ogre is:

○ Answer 1: the kind ruler of the hobgoblin kingdom, where all hobgoblins live in peace and harmony with the elves, trolls, and fairies.

○ Answer 2: a huge monster with a horned head.

○ Answer 3: a naughty brownie.

○ Answer 4: the king of dwarves.

✤ 4 ✤
Who Are *Your*
Favorite Characters?

Everyone has a favorite *Spiderwick* character. I have my own favorite character in the *Spiderwick* books, and if you read on, you'll find out who that is. . . .

Jared. Jared might be the greatest character because everyone dumps on him yet he saves the day. It must be really hard to do that. Most kids would want to give up if everyone was always blaming them for everything that went wrong. Even Jared's mother blames him for everything that goes wrong. And he's failing in school, and he's really depressed because his father left the family and now they're really poor and miserable. Still, somehow, Jared manages to save everybody from real evil. And he's funny!

Simon. Simon's kind of cool because he's quiet and scared of a lot of things, yet he has a really good heart. He saves animals all the time, and he even saves Byron, the giant griffin bird. Also, Simon stands by Jared through thick and thin, defending his twin brother when Jared is accused of doing all the bad things that Thimbletack is really doing. It's hard to say whether I like Jared better than Simon or Simon better than Jared.

Mallory. She's tough and strong, and she's very athletic. But she isn't mean, and usually in books when girls are really strong and tough, they can be mean, too. Mallory seems to like her twin brothers. She doesn't pick on them. She doesn't torment them. Lots of older sisters torment their younger brothers all the time. I think it's cool that Mallory is a fencing champion, too. But I don't know why girls in books can't be really strong and tough but also act like standard girls, too.

Aunt Lucinda. One of my favorite characters is Aunt Lucinda. I think it's really awesome how she's lived with fairies her whole life, and I'd like to do that, too. I want to eat fairy fruits and see what they taste like. Forget watermelons. Forget apples. Even forget cherries. I bet fairy fruits are a lot better than anything, even candy and pizza. I don't want to be as old as Aunt Lucinda. Not ever. But I'd like to see what it's like to be her for a while, maybe when she was a lot younger.

Thimbletack the House Brownie. Thimbletack is my favorite character. He's both playful and kind, while at the same time naughty and overly sensitive. I sense that Thimbletack really has a heart of gold and wants to help, but he also wants to have his way and be free of people. He's a shape-shifter, which means he can turn from his brownie-boggart form into a lizard, rat, or eel, and probably a lot of other creatures. He's loads of fun, no matter what he's doing, and I love the pictures of him.

Fast Fact Quiz!

A dumbwaiter is:

○ Answer 1: a really stupid guy who serves you soup instead of cheesecake.

○ Answer 2: a basketlike device that moves between floors in a house.

○ Answer 3: a really stupid guy who serves you liver instead of ice cream.

○ Answer 4: a really stupid guy who serves you radish sandwiches instead of grilled cheese.

A Story About the Hobgoblin Puck

Puck is a famous hobgoblin type of fairy. He's a very mischievous nature spirit who often lives in houses. He goes by many names, including Poake, Pwca, Robin Goodfellow, Puckle, and Pug. In addition to being called a hobgoblin, he's called by other fairy names, too: brownie, elf, gobbling. Because he can shape-shift, it's thought that people can't figure out his true fairy nature. But most people say that Puck is of human shape and very small. He's certainly had an excellent career in the theater, appearing in plays as famous as Shakespeare's *A Midsummer Night's Dream.* In the play, he is shown as a playful sprite who embarrasses people by leading them into uncomfortable situations. But he's also kind to the poor, the lovesick, and the needy. As with many fairies, Puck has two sides: impish and full of pranks; good-natured and full of love.

Hobgoblins are closely related to brownies. They are usually drawn by artists as looking like ugly, little elves. They help humans do household chores, just like their brownie cousins. Although hobgoblins share the "goblins" part of their names with the evil goblins, the two are quite different: hobgoblins are good-natured and kind, though easily offended by what humans do. Brownies are easily offended by what humans do, too.

At any rate, the hobgoblin Puck is one of the most famous fairies of all time. He is the personal attendant to Oberon, the Fairy King of the Otherworld. Oberon is a dwarf with a beautiful face, and he likes to tramp around the English woods playing pranks on humans. With him on these escapades are all his fairy sprites, led by Puck. Oberon particularly enjoys luring humans into Fairyland, where he can keep them for centuries. Do you remember Rip van Winkle, who was asleep for twenty years? I bet he was really in Fairyland.

Puck is often said to be a phooka, a shape-shifter who would sometimes turn himself into a horse, only to lead people on wild rides into the water, where he dumped them. The Welsh Puck would carry a lantern while showing people the way through the night woods, then blow out the light when near the edge of a cliff.

✦ 5 ✦
Magical Beings

One of the most interesting aspects of *The Spiderwick Chronicles* is that it contains magical creatures of all kinds. Jared, Simon, and Mallory encounter goblins, griffins, fairies (including brownies, pixies, sprites, and boggarts), dwarves, dragons, elves, ogres, unicorns, and trolls, among others. While the next chapter offers some tips for identifying magical creatures that match your personality and that you might want to be, this chapter tells you the truth about all these strange beasts.

Are they real?

Well, what do *you* think?

There's a woman named Gossamer Penwyche (which you must admit is one of the most beautiful names you've ever heard), and in her book, *The World of Fairies,* she writes, "I believe in fairies. My belief is based on a simple, childlike faith that I have never lost and a childhood experience I have never forgotten." Much like Jared, Simon, and Mallory, Gossamer Penwyche encountered fairies when she was a child. It was summer, and she was in the woods, playing in a stream near her house. While she was daydreaming with her legs floating in the water, the wind picked up and blew around her like a minitornado, birds started chirping, a hawk screamed then grew quiet. Gossamer Penwyche heard children's laughter and singing, but when she looked around, nobody was there. The hawk dove at her face, and she fell into the water, only to hear the children laughing more loudly, presumably at her. She eventually realized that hours had passed rather than minutes and that she'd just experienced a spell of intense magic. She was certain she'd heard the laughter and songs of fairies.[3]

But that's just one person. Have other people encountered fairies?

The famous fairy artist Sulamith Wulfing writes, "My ideas come to me from many sources, and in such harmony with my personal experiences that I can turn them into these fairy compositions."[4]

Fairies are usually shown in books and paintings as tiny, winged people with the ability to do magical things. They're kind and playful. We all know about the tooth fairy, for example, who flutters into our bedrooms at night and gives us coins (or other small gifts) for the teeth we've left under our pillows. Then there's the fairy

---

[3]Gossamer Penwyche, *The World of Fairies,* New York: Sterling Publishing, 2001, pp. 6–7.

[4]David Larkin, *The Fantastic Art of Sulamith Wulfing,* New York: Peacock/Bantam, 1978; quoted at http://www.bpip.com/wulfing.htm.

godmother, who is often depicted as a human-sized, winged elderly woman of great kindness.

Like most children, you've probably tried to figure out if the tooth fairy is real or if she's just your mother pretending to be a tooth fairy. When my son, Dan, was in elementary school and losing teeth, I'd flap my arms as if they were wings and tiptoe-dance into his bedroom late at night when I thought he was asleep. I did this arm-flapping-and-tiptoe-dancing routine even though I knew he was asleep. Don't ask me why. Maybe I'm just weird. At any rate, I would take his lost tooth from beneath his pillow and leave a quarter in its place. He always asked if I was the tooth fairy. If I had minded my own business and not flap-danced into his room at night, maybe the *real* tooth fairy would have come instead.

When I was a girl, I tried to stay awake long enough to catch my mother playing the role of the tooth fairy. But I never caught her.

It never occurred to me to try and trick the

tooth fairy, aka my mother (if indeed my mother *was* the tooth fairy), to discover the truth about lost teeth, quarters, and fairies. Without lying, what can you possibly do to get to the bottom of this matter?

Well, one thing you can do is put a lost tooth under your pillow but not tell your mother that you've even lost the tooth. If she says something funny or she happens to be in the room when a friend of yours says something funny, force yourself not to laugh. If you open your mouth, your mother could notice the lost tooth. And then she'll know that a tooth might be under your pillow that night.

Now if you lose a tooth and don't tell your mother, but you can't help laughing and she notices that you have a new, gaping hole between your teeth, put the tooth under your mattress instead of under your pillow. Now try really hard to stay awake long enough to see who comes into your room at night to look for the tooth.

I know: I'm talking a lot about the tooth fairy, but let's face it, she's the fairy we encounter most often in our lives, isn't she? Do we have a toenail fairy? No. Do we have a belly button fairy? No. We have *only* a tooth fairy. So either we prove she exists or we're out of luck in determining whether fairies are real.

Unless, of course, you happen to see tiny, winged creatures flitting around your teacher's head or over the refrigerator. If this is the case, write to me, because I want to know if you've actually seen real fairies.

I'm going to talk only a tiny bit more about the tooth fairy, then shift to other things. Have you wondered how the tooth fairy knows you've lost a tooth? Does she have lost-tooth radar? Do your teeth emit supersonic transmissions that only the tooth fairy can detect? Do your parents have a special hotline telephone that connects directly to her at any time of the day or night? Also, where does she get all the money that she puts under kids' pillows? Say, ten million kids lose a total of twenty million teeth in one year. I got only a quarter for my teeth, but that was in the olden days, so we'll assume that today's fairy leaves a dollar per tooth. That would mean the fairy leaves twenty million dollars a year beneath pillows. Where does this twenty million dollars come from? Does the tooth fairy rob banks? Is she connected to the mob? Does she have a private money printing press? As my final thought about this particular fairy, I'll note that somehow, the tooth fairy can magically leave money in any currency used on the planet. If you're a kid in Thailand, she'll leave you bahts. If you're in Ireland, you'll get euros. If you're in Japan, you'll get yen. And so on. How on earth does she keep track of all this and get the right kinds of money on the very day some kid loses a tooth?

Very perplexing.

My guess is that there are tens of millions of tooth fairies in the world, and they're all in an interconnected Tooth Fairy Network. If some kid loses a tooth in India, one of ten thousand Indian tooth fairies handles the job. And all these tooth fairies have a huge repository of lost teeth hidden beneath the Earth's surface. After all, they have to put all those teeth somewhere. There are probably two hundred thousand trillion lost teeth stashed away somewhere beneath your house.

Belief in magical creatures, such as tooth fairies, is as old as mankind. The belief died off as formal religions took hold, but within the past hundred years or so, belief in fairies has started to rise again. People are still reporting that they see fairies. As depicted in books and painting, the fairies are usually called *good people,* even though they're also thought to be somewhat rambunctious (meaning unruly and hard to control). In real life, as in *The Spiderwick Chronicles,* fairies are considered to be shape-shifters by those who believe in them.

Fairies supposedly live in mounds (small

hills). Time flows at a different pace in Fairy-land than in our world. If you spend an hour in Fairyland and then return to our world, you suddenly might be ten years older. In the case of Arthur Spiderwick and other people who enter Fairyland, they don't age at all, yet when they return to the real world, they're the same age they would have been had they never left.

Belief in fairies is worldwide. People have debated the origins of fairies for centuries. There are people who spend their lives studying the subject, and they even get college degrees in folklore, which includes the study of all things magical. Some scholars think that fairies originated when long-ago people believed in many powerful gods and goddesses. When these powerful gods and goddesses started dying off in religion, they remained in people's minds as fairies, sprites, and other magical beings.

Some people think that fairies are really angels who were rejected from heaven but weren't evil enough for hell. In addition to the Old and New Testaments, commonly known as the Bible, angels are found in the Book of Mormon, the Koran, and the Dead Sea Scrolls. Many religions incorporate angels into their theology.

In the ancient period between A.D. 1 and A.D. 500, the Roman world was one of pagan polytheism and emperor worship. Early Christians, following the examples set by the Romans and others, often worshiped angels. People thought that angels were perfect beings created by God and that their bodies were made of light.

During the second century A.D., the Gnostics believed in two gods, one good and the other evil. In addition, they believed that spirit was good and matter was not. From the good god, the spiritual one, emanated a vast number of angels.

But for the most part, people have believed that fairies are simple spirits of nature, not fallen angels. These spirits are manifestations of animal and human souls and thoughts. This means that the fairies are created from some essence of our spirits that is everywhere at all times.

In the 1400s, a man named Paracelsus classified fairies into four groups. The fairies who live in the air are called *sylphs.* Those who live on earth are *gnomes.* The underwater fairies are called *undines,* and, finally, the fairies who deal with fire are the *salamanders.*

The gnomes may be dryads, hamadryads (tree spirits), brownies, elves, satyrs, or goblins. They're concerned mainly with rocks, stones, plants, minerals, and gems. When working with animals or humans, they handle the bones. If betrayed, earth elementals, or gnomes, are vengeful and cause a lot of trouble. Lore has it that gnomes guard treasures, such as pots of gold.

The air elementals, or sylphs, cast the winds and make the snow and clouds. Sometimes they cause dreams, and within humans and animals, they work within the realms of the nervous system. Generally, the sylphs are happy spirits, dancing in the grass and on the flowers, and they tend to be generous and kind.

The fire elementals, or salamanders, are directly responsible for fire: without these elementals, fire cannot be created. Within humans and animals, they work within the realms of the bloodstream and the liver, and they affect human emotions. Salamanders look either like lizards or like tiny balls of light in the middle of a flame.

The water elementals are made up of the undines, water sprites, mermaids, sea nymphs, and such strange-sounding creatures as limoniades, nereides, potamides, oreades, and naiads. As you may have guessed, they create ocean waves and guard other bodies of water, such as lakes and rivers. People believe that a water elemental guards each fountain, each creek, each spurt of water. Undines are physically beautiful beings, most often considered female, and they often take on human form to communicate and interact with people.

Paracelsus believed that all fairies are made of flesh and blood, just like humans, and that they have many of the attributes of humans. But, he said, fairies live much longer than humans and their souls do not exist forever.

In the 1600s, Robert Kirk, a Scotsman, wrote that fairies exist in a plane somewhere between humans and angels. He described fairy bodies in a way that many people still use to describe angel bodies: light, shape-shifting into different forms, and twinkling like little, condensed, starlike people.[5]

Even today there are scholars who claim that the sun itself is a conscious entity, and for proof we need only consider the fact that our own mental activity "is associated with complex electromagnetic patterns in our brains." Because the sun is highly sensitive to electromagnetism, it's possible for the sun itself to think, to dream,

---

[5]Robert Kirt, *The Secret Commonwealth of Elves, Fauns and Fairies,* 1691.

and to be full of cosmic consciousness.[6] Indeed, if the sun is conscious, then all the other stars might be conscious, as well. And the stars might hold the angels within them; in fact, the intelligence of the stars might be the angels themselves.[7] If you believe that the stars are angels and that the sun is conscious and thinks, then it's a simple step to believe in fairies. And we're talking about scientists who believe these things.

It is generally believed by many people that angels communicate with one another through some form of mental telepathy. In addition, most people who believe in angels think that angels travel instantaneously and can be anywhere at any given time. It's easy to see why people link angels and fairies.

In the 1800s, people called Spiritualists di-

---

[6]Matthew Fox, Ph.D., an Episcopal priest, and Rupert Sheldrake, Ph.D., a biologist, in *The Physics of Angels: Exploring the Realm Where Science and Spirit Meet*, San Francisco: HarperSanFrancisco, 1996, pp. 18–19.

[7]*Ibid.*, p. 20.

vided the fairies into two types. The first type consisted of nature spirits who were tied to trees, rivers, forests, lakes, and other forms of nature. The second type consisted of angellike fairies who dwelled somewhere between thought and matter.[8]

In the early 1900s, Charles W. Leadbeater took Charles Darwin's theory of evolution (which you'll learn about in school, hopefully) and used it to classify fairies the same way that scientists classify animals and plants. He wrote that Fairyland consists of seven distinct areas and that fairies occupied England before humans lived there. According to Leadbeater, humans took over England and drove out the fairies, who evolved in order to cope. In fact, they evolved from water up through fungi and bacteria and further through reptiles, birds, and eventually, to the spiritual plane. At this spiritual level, as

---

[8]Spiritualists believed in psychic mediums who could contact the dead and other supernatural beings. If a medium could talk to a dead guy, why not talk to a fairy?

full mature fairies, they were linked to the air, earth, water, and fire. Even as fully mature fairies, they continued to evolve until they were indeed like angels and existed as solar spirits.

Other ideas about fairies lived alongside the ideas that the creatures were angels, spirits, and similar to humans. For example, a fairy researcher named Edward Gardner believed that fairies were like butterflies and made from something that's even lighter than air. This is why, claimed Gardner, fairies are invisible except as the mere twinkling of light. Gardner thought that fairies linked plants and sunlight. If not for fairies, plants couldn't grow.

Even medical doctors had their notions about fairies. Dr. Franz Hartmann, who studied fairies and translated a fairy book called *Philosophia Occulta*, believed that fairies lived inside people as well as throughout nature. Fairies helped our bodies function correctly.

Long ago, the Welsh people thought that Fairyland was in the mountains to the north of them. Later, they thought that Fairyland was on a rocky peninsula; and still later, they believed that the fairies were on an island. Sailors would see the island, and at later times claim that the island had disappeared. The British called this place The Isle of Man. The Irish called it Hy Breasail.

Of all the fairy islands, Avalon is the best known, for it was to Avalon that King Arthur was taken when he was mortally wounded. The story of King Arthur and the knights of his Round Table is very well known.

As in *Spiderwick,* fairy tales in the real world include mention of fairy foods, such as fruits. According to these tales, if a person eats a fairy food, he won't be able to eat regular food again. Aunt Lucinda has this problem in the *Spiderwick* books, and hence, she's dwindling into a mere fragment of Aunt Lucinda: she's wispy-thin.

You probably haven't read any Shakespearean plays yet. He was a very famous writer of long ago, and you'll have to study his plays in school. One of his plays is called *A Midsummer Night's Dream*, and in it, Shakespeare features a lot of fairies, including the king and queen of fairies, Oberon and Titania, as well as the hobgoblin Puck.

Most fairies are mischievous and tricky. Rather than leave money for teeth, most fairies will take the teeth and leave mildew under your pillow, just because it amuses them to do this to you. Yet when someone is poor or really sick, most fairies will try to help by using their magic.

Further, according to legend, fairies live in two types of communities, based on what they like to do and how they interact with humans. Peaceful fairies who mind their own business and don't cause much trouble for people reside in something known as the Seelie Court. They emerge in forests and fields to dance amongst the flowers and ferns, to feast, and to sing. Fairies who are dangerous to people and want to cause lots of trouble reside in the Unseelie

Court, ruled by the dark queen Nicnivin. These types of fairies live in the true wilderness and should be avoided at all cost. So if you're ever lost in the true wilderness—in the Amazon jungle, for example—and you see a tiny, winged guy slapping a monkey around, run!

In England, a book called *The Faerie Queene,* first published in 1590, was actually dedicated to the Queen of England. Shakespeare, whom I mentioned a few paragraphs ago, was an English author. And a guy named Poole followed Shakespeare's *Midsummer Night's Dream* with a story in 1657 about fairies, including the famous Tom Thumb, and hobgoblins.

Tom Thumb first appeared in print in a pamphlet written by Richard Johnson in 1621. In a 1630 adaptation of Johnson's story, a farmer and his wife desperately wanted a child, and they asked Merlin, King Arthur's sorcerer, to help them. Even if the child was as small a thumb, they told Merlin, they would love the baby with all their hearts. Naturally, Merlin conjured up a little boy who was the size of a thumb, and his name was Tom Thumb. Being a tiny fairy child, Tom Thumb got into all sorts of trouble. Only his fairy magic saved him, time and time again. The female version of Tom Thumb is the fairy girl, Thumbelina.

In English tales, fairies often live underground where ancient stone circles are found. Or they're found in Fairyland, where they dance, play music, and party, inviting humans they've befriended. I don't know about you, but I'd think twice about going to Fairyland for a party. For one thing, it would be hard to fit inside a near-microscopic blob of dirt or a rock. And it wouldn't be much of a party if I had to eat a crumb rather than a cupcake, drink a half drop of juice instead of a glass of soda.

In Ireland, fairies are known as Daoine Sidhe, and the Irish people say that fairies are really fallen angels who once were gods. Most Irish fairies belong to a supernatural race called the Tuatha de Danaan, and the legendary acts of these supernatural beings are recorded in medieval texts with names such as *Dun Cow, Lismore,* and *Lecan.* As in England, the Irish fairies live in mounds of dirt and stone circles. They might also live in Irish lakes. The fairy kings have various names, among them, Finvarra and Dagda. The fairy queens have names such as Cliodna, Aynia, Onagh, Aoibhinn, and Aine. Some of the most famous Irish fairies are leprechauns and banshees.

Leprechauns make and mend shoes. If your shoe needs a new sole, a leprechaun could sneak into your closet, grab the shoe while you're asleep, put a new sole on it, and then return it before you wake up. Actually, the leprechaun's original name was *luchorpan,* which means "little body." A long time ago, a luchorpan was also thought to be a dwarf. The typical leprechaun is constantly hammering away at shoes, so if you hear constant tapping in your walls, you may have a leprechaun in the house. He guards crocks of gold, too, and he plays pranks on humans all the time. So if you happen to see gold nuggets in your bathroom, you might be living with a leprechaun. And if the gold nuggets turn out to be fool's gold (a nongold ore, similar in color to gold, that is often mistaken for the real thing), you *definitely* have a leprechaun in the house.

A **banshee** is a "woman of the fairy mound" and comes from the Irish words *bean* (meaning "woman") and *si* (meaning "fairy mound," "fairy," or just "mound"). She's an elderly woman in a long, green dress, and if she wails under your window, she's letting you know that you might soon die. As you might have guessed, the banshee has red eyes from crying so much. It's a tough thing to go through your entire life just wailing under the windows of people who are about to die.

In Scotland, female fairies are both gorgeous and evil. The Scottish fairy queen rides a horse that has silver bells braided into its mane, and as most fairies do, she wears green clothes. Scottish fairies live in the moors and mountains, and just like fairies everywhere, they like to dance, play music, and have parties. During the winter nights, the Unseelie Court fairies emerge and cause trouble, so Scottish people who believe in fairies stay inside.

Spanish fairies are known as *fada,* from the Latin word *fatum,* which means "fate." It is said that Spanish fairies can control fate using magic. They live in houses and are malicious and vindictive.

French fairies are also called *fées.* Notice how similar this word—as well as the Spanish *fada*—is to Thimbletack's use of the word *fey* to describe fairies. Most French fairies are female and thought to be full of kindness.

As in Spain, the Italian fairies are also called *fada,* but in this case, the *fada* are divided into many different kinds of nymphs.

Nymphs are very tiny female nature spirits and appear most often in Greece and Rome. A nymph is a beautiful young girl dressed in a silky, translucent gown. Her hair is gorgeous, she looks like a goddess, and she spends her time playing musical instruments, dancing, and delivering prophesies to humans.

There are fairies *all over* the world, not only in the places named above but also in Lithuania, Malaysia, Nigeria, Hungary, Germany, Iran, Scandinavia, Albania, and even China. However, there are many *different kinds* of fairies. Many are in the *Spiderwick* books; others aren't mentioned at all.

For example, **spriggan** fairies aren't mentioned in *Spiderwick*. These are ugly, little creatures who can turn themselves into huge, hideous monsters. They guard treasures in the hills and operate as thieves and bandits. They create whirlwinds that destroy fields, and they rob human houses.

Gwragedd Annwn, who are Welsh water fairies,

don't appear in *Spiderwick,* either. These are beautiful female lake fairies who sometimes marry human men. Perhaps they marry really short human men who weigh less than fifty pounds.

Nor do we see thrummy caps, thrumpins, kulshedras, kurinyi bogs (spirits who live in rocks and guard family hens), fachans, fad felens (disease spirits whose golden eyes cause horrible illnesses), mirus, or tuas (a snakelike spirit, created when a person dreams, who helps the dreamer through life).

Goblins are nasty little creatures who dwell in Fairyland. They're ugly as sin, they steal anything they can get their claws on, and they like to lure people to certain death by dangling fairy fruits and other items in front of them.

Goblins are known by various names, such as *gobblings* and *gobelines.* When standing, the top of a goblin's head might reach your knee. He usually doesn't look like a frog as in *Spiderwick,* but rather he appears as an old man with a long, gray beard. Goblins generally like children and give them presents and treats, but the goblins dislike adults and tend to disrupt households by wrecking kitchens and furniture.

The household goblin of legend is much like the *Spiderwick* boggart-brownie Thimbletack. Legends also explain that to rid your house of a goblin, you must spread flaxseed on the floors. Because goblins can't resist counting and ordering things—just like Thimbletack!—they will stop everything to pick up and count all the flaxseed. Eventually, the goblins will get so tired that they'll leave your house to find a place that doesn't have flaxseed all over the floors. I'm not sure why flaxseed is specified, as it seems likely that any type of small seed will do.

Fairy tales do tell of evil goblins who live and work in mines, just as the dwarves dwell and work in the quarries of *Spiderwick.*

The mine-dwelling goblins are called *knockers* because they're always knocking on the walls of the quarries seeking rich minerals and gems. In Germany, the knockers are known as *kobolds* and *wichtlein*. Of course, other societies have knockers, as well.

In traditional fairy lore, a house **brownie** is also called a *little man, dobie, bogle, hobs, domovoi, bodach, nis, killmoulis, chin-chin kobakama, tomtra,* and *yumboes,* among many other names. Just like Thimbletack, the standard brownie is a shaggy, very short man. He wears a ragged suit and small cap.

The brownie does indeed adopt a house, and he emerges at night to do chores or cause problems. Brownies, according to real-life tradition, do like bowls of milk, just like Thimbletack in *Spiderwick*.

It is said that brownies are easily offended by what humans do. For example, if a person leaves too much milk in a bowl for the household brownie, the brownie may get really upset and leave the house forever.

One story tells of an old house that belonged to the Macdonald family to the west of Cantyre. This old house had a brownie who drank way too much milk and shrieked a lot when he got hurt in the walls. Because the brownie lived in a Macdonald house—and all Macdonalds supposedly hated all Campbells because of a famous battle between the two clans—this particular household brownie hated all Campbells.

On the other side of Cantyre was an old Macdonald castle, which also had a household brownie (or castle brownie, I suppose). The castle was built long before the old house on the west side of Cantyre. As soon as the house was built, the castle brownie disappeared forever, and suddenly, a house brownie appeared in the new Macdonald home.

Many people had heard this brownie in the house, but nobody had ever really seen him. He did clean the house, including the sheets and clothes. If somebody made too much of a mess in the house, then after that person went to sleep at night, the brownie would slap him silly. In fact, messy people would wake up the next morning with bruises all over their faces. Because this brownie killed dogs at night, the owners of the house always made sure that their dogs were outside all night long.

Now the **boggarts** are ill-tempered, mean, ugly-as-sin brownies. They completely destroy everything they don't like. They are shape-shifters and can take many different forms, such as a sheep, a dog, a goat, a tree, or your favorite pair of jeans. (Always look inside your jeans before you put them on. You wouldn't want to go to school wearing a household boggart.)

Boggarts who materialize in human form are far more dangerous than boggarts who appear in other forms (unless, of course, they appear as your jeans, your toothbrush, or your father's shaving cream). Boggarts play tricks, but they also scare and hurt people. They trip people in the kitchen, which can be pretty dangerous if the stove is on. They trip people in the shower. They yank blankets off you at night so you freeze in the winter, and in the summer you might wake up on a humid, 100-degree morning to find yourself plastered to the bed beneath fourteen heavy winter comforters.

There's an old story about a boggart and a farmer: A farmer decides to leave his home and land in hopes that he can finally be rid of the household boggart. The farmer gathers his wife, his mother, and his sixteen children. They pack all their belongings. They have no idea what's in store for them, and their only hope is to be done with the nasty boggart who's been giving them heat rashes in the summer and pneumonia in the winter. As they reach the outer gate of the farm, some loitering neighbors ask where the family is heading. Before the farmer, his wife, his mother, or any of his sixteen children can answer, a voice pipes up from within the mountain of family bedding: "Aye, we're flittin' this place." The boggart is still with them, and realizing they can never escape his grasp, the family returns to the farm, unpacks, and lives unhappily ever after.

Dwarves are small, and they look like misshapen humans. They usually have long, gray beards and look really old. They are also miners, according to legend, so their role in *Spiderwick* conforms to what we know about dwarves. Rumors say that dwarves are toads during the day. (This sounds a lot like the goblins in *Spiderwick*.) If the dwarves are hit by sunlight, they turn to stone. According to folklore, dwarves turn metal into beautiful but dangerous artifacts. These artifacts possess spells and curses. The dwarves are often invisible because they wear magic clothing.

As you might have guessed, there are many types of dwarves in the real world, and overall they are considered to be a type of goblin. On the island of Rugen in the Baltic Sea, people identify three types of dwarves based solely on the color of their clothes—white, brown, or black.

The white dwarves are kind and gentle, and they spend their time mining gold and silver from underground caverns. In the summer, they dance in the form of butterflies.

The brown dwarves act much like boggarts, but they steal babies (very bad behavior!) while causing a lot of other troubles for people.

The black dwarves are pure evil. They're ugly, too. (Have you ever wondered why all the evil magical beings are ugly, while the nice magical beings are beautiful and handsome? Why can't we have a beautiful yet evil black dwarf, or an ugly yet kindhearted nymph?) The black dwarves use false lights to lure treasure-laden ships to shore, then the dwarves attack the ships and steal the treasures. They make deadly weapons out of ore that they mine, which is a lot worse than making artifacts that cast spells. When not killing and stealing, the black dwarves turn into owls that screech constantly.

A very well known creation story comes from Iceland and Scandinavia. In this story, dwarves end up holding the entire world in place.

The Norse people recorded their beliefs in what is called the *Younger* (or prose) *Edda*, written by Snorri Sturluson in approximately 1220. Sturluson based his *Younger Edda* on the oral (spoken) myths of the *Elder* (or poetic) *Edda*. In this story, the world was created from the body of the evil ice giant, Ymir.

As the story goes, King Gylfi, who ruled what we now call Sweden, learned about the Aesir, the gods of Valhalla. Gylfi disguised himself and went to Valhalla to meet the High One and learn all about the Aesir and the beginning of the world.

The High One explained that there were two atmospheres, one in the north, the other in the south. The northern atmosphere was dark and icy; the southern was light and warm. Between the two atmospheres was total emptiness, called

Ginnungagap. Within the void of Ginnungagap, the cold northern air mingled with the
warm southern air, creating moisture, and
hence, life began to form. The first form of life
was the evil ice giant called Ymir.

Ymir was alone in Ginnungagap, but he lay
down, and while resting, his armpits gave birth to
a man and a woman, and his legs mated to create
a son. A family of ogres was born. As the ice
melted in Ginnungagap, it turned into a cow giant named Auohumla, whose milk turned into
nutritious rivers. A man arose from some ice that
Auohumla was licking, and he was Buri the
Strong, whose son Bor married Bestla, a daughter of the original ogres. Bor and Bestla had a
child, the great god Odin, as well as other children, the gods Vili and Ve. These gods rose up
and killed Ymir the evil ice giant, and then took
the giant's corpse to the middle of Ginnungagap,
where they transformed his blood into the oceans
and his body into the earth. Mountains formed

from his bones, rocks and trees from his teeth. His brains became the clouds. Ymir's skull became the top of the sky and was held up in the north, south, east, and west by four dwarves.

The Scandinavians say that the dwarves were created by maggots that crawled from Ymir's body and that there are three types of dwarves. The first is a group called Modsognir's folk, the second is Durin's group, and the third is known as having descended from Dwalin's alliance with Lovar. The dwarves make magic spears, ships, and other objects—even magic hair.

Pixies are fairies who look like hedgehogs, and they are also called piskies, pigseys, and pisgies. They steal horses and ride across the moors at night, screaming in delight. They are sometimes thought to be pookas and pucks. The pixies usually look like tiny children with red hair and pointed ears, and if you give them new clothes, they feel compelled to leave your house. So if you're not sure if you have a brownie living with you or a pixie, give him a gift of new clothes. If he's a brownie, he'll still be around in the morning. If he's a pixie, he'll leave you forever.

In *The Spiderwick Chronicles: Lucinda's Secret (Book Three of Five)* Jared describes **phookas** as looking like monkeys with speckled, black-brown fur and long tails. The *Spiderwick* phooka has long tufts of fur around its neck and a rabbit's face with rabbit ears and whiskers. Jared explains to Simon and Mallory that phookas are shape-shifters.

It is true that phookas are sometimes considered Irish goblins who assume the shapes of various strange mythical creatures and beasts. According to some stories, phookas sport black fur, feathers, and skin. So Jared's phooka could indeed look like a monkey with speckled fur and a rabbit's head.

According to most legends, however, phookas are monstrous water horses who haunt streams and lakes, trying to entice victims to mount them. If someone mounts a phooka, the beast bolts into the water or over a cliff, sending its rider to his death.

According to Hogsqueal, Mulgarath's lair is a palace of trash in a dump, and it is defended by dragons. Later, Arthur explains that Mulgarath's dragons are probably of the wyrm type common to their part of the world, and that wyrm dragons are very poisonous.

What is a **dragon**? Are dragons kind, evil, helpful to mankind, or destructive?

Although stories and myths about dragons reach far back into history, there is no evidence that dragons ever existed. However, it is possible that giant creatures existed with some of the traits of dragons.

In approximately 5,000 B.C., stories described a Sumerian dragon named Zu. This dragon stole some tablets from Enlil, a god who enlisted the sun-god Ninurta to get the tablets back and kill Zu.

Another common type of dragon was the sea

monster, which, like land-based dragons, fought gods. For example, Enuma Elish, which is an early Babylonian myth, spoke of the dragons Apsu (the name means "fresh water") and Tiamat (the name means "salt sea"). These two dragons begot the first gods, which in turn begot all creatures. In the Canaanite Poem of Baal, a young god defeated the seven-headed sea dragon, Yam-Nahar. An early Egyptian story told of the sea dragon, Apophis, trying to kill the Egyptian sun god Ra.

Chinese dragons are much nicer than Western dragons, such as the ones in *Spiderwick*. The Chinese dragons come in four main forms: Tien-Lung, the Celestial Dragon, who protects the places where gods live: Shen-Lung, the Spiritual Dragon, who controls rains and other storms; Ti-Lung, the Earth Dragon, who controls rivers; and Fut-Lung, the Underworld Dragon, who guards treasures.

Dragons of all kinds have been taken very seriously throughout Chinese history. Five-toed dragons were a symbol of great power and supposedly spoke directly to the gods. Only the Chinese emperors were "allowed" to communicate with these five-toed Imperial Dragons, and the penalty to citizens of attempting discourse with a five-toed dragon was death.

It has been postulated that the ancient belief in dragons stemmed from the discovery of dinosaur bones. It is conceivable that giant creatures were unearthed from their graves and that ancient people believed them to have been dragons. However, written records of dragons precede any discovery of prehistoric remains.

Interesting as all this is, let's consider the wyrm dragon, for this is the type of dragon guarding the *Spiderwick* trash dump. Because the wyrm dragons live in the trash dump, they are probably not Underworld Dragons, guarding buried jewels and other treasures. Yes, I know that some people regard trash as treasure—

Mulgarath is probably one of those people, I mean, ogres—but it's unlikely that the wyrms consider themselves guardians of jewels, gold, and other true treasures. Also, these dragons do not create great tempests and floods, so they probably aren't Spiritual Dragons or Earth Dragons. Nor do they appear to be protecting a place where gods live, unless all of a sudden an ogre is a god, which I highly doubt!

The word *wyrm* comes from the Norse word for dragon, which sounds like *worm, orm,* or *vurm.* This type of dragon lives where the Vikings invaded the northeastern parts of the British Isles more than a thousand years ago. The wyrm dragon has no wings, and his red scaled body is snakelike. His head looks like a cross between a dragon's head and a horse's head. Sometimes he has horns. He *always* has fangs. Of course, he breathes fire, though he's also been known to breathe malodorous (which means "horribly smelly") fumes. A wyrm dragon is always pure evil. He lives in smelly, stinking, rotting places such as swamps and trash dumps.

As for **elves,** Norse myths tell of Light Elves, the Liosalfar, who live high in the sky and are compassionate and kind. The Dark Elves, or Dockalfar, on the other hand, live beneath the ground and are nasty creatures. According to standard fairy lore, elves are pretty tall compared to most fairies, who are so small we can barely see them. Elves stand from 4'10" to 5'8" or more. They're slim and delicate, with huge eyes of beautiful colors.

The three elves in *Spiderwick* conform to this traditional look. They are Mallory's height. The female elf has apple green eyes. The other two are male elves. The first has deep green skin, and the other has red berries woven in his bright red hair. In fact, all three *Spiderwick* elves are beautiful, just in different ways. They are creatures of the forest.

The *Spiderwick* elves are probably Light Elves

rather than Dark Elves. For one thing, they aren't at all evil. They want The Field Guide so humans will stop driving them from the forests to their death. Again, this is right along the lines of standard fairy literature ranging way back through the centuries. For another, the *Spiderwick* elves aren't pitch-black like the traditional Dark Elves, and their eyes aren't fluorescent. And finally, the *Spiderwick* elves live in the forest, where Light Elves are said to dwell. Dark Elves live in underground caves.

Furthermore, according to folklore, Light Elves are seen only in special places where nature is undisturbed. They play music and they love art. Older elves are wiser and even more delicate and beautiful than younger elves. The elves are calm and patient, and they live for a very long time. All of these descriptions of Light Elves in real life could just as easily be descriptions of *Spiderwick* elves.

Trolls have lots of different names. Around

the world, they are known as *berg people, jutul, tusse, hill men,* and *trows,* among others. Belief in trolls began in Germany and Scandinavia, but trolls are found all over the world. Supposedly, trolls guard bridges and byways. They don't guard these places for good reasons, either. Usually, trolls hide beneath the bridges, then jump out and scare people half to death, demanding huge amounts of money and treasure, sometimes even human life. The troll in *Spiderwick* guards a stream and is described as huge, with a green head, tiny black eyes, nasty-looking teeth, and long, gnarled fingers.

In the real world, the Scandinavian people believe that trolls are giants, and that the biggest troll, Dovregubben, who lives in the Dovre mountain, is their king. Trolls have rough hair and mossy growths on their heads, just like the *Spiderwick* troll. One funny thing about trolls is that they supposedly can stir soups with their long noses.

Trolls live a long time, just like other creatures of Fairyland, but sunlight turns trolls into stone. Some trolls have multiple heads, and some only have one eye, which sits in the middle of their foreheads.

Just as in *Spiderwick*, trolls are easily tricked. Jared easily outsmarts the troll when he points out that goblins are juicy and fat. The troll forgets about Jared's brother and sister, enabling the three children to escape. Trolls may look mean, but they're pretty simpleminded and naïve.

Ogres are giants born from a merging of Orcus, the Roman god of death and darkness, and Saturn, a god who supposedly ate Hungarian tribes for dessert. Ogres have ugly faces, lots of body hair, and they have big humps on their backs. They smell like garbage, which is probably why the *Spiderwick* ogre lives in a trash dump. Many ogres wear enchanted boots, which enable them to run quickly. Ogres are thieves and will steal anything.

One famous ogre is the giant in "Jack and the

Beanstalk." That ogre will eat anything, including humans—probably entire countries of humans with a few Hungarian tribes for dessert—as well as five thousand hot dogs, forty-five thousand chickens, and six million loaves of bread.

Griffins are basically huge mythical birds. Some stories say that griffins are part bird and part lion; others describe griffins that are mostly lions with eagles' heads. When a griffin is mostly lion, it often doesn't even have wings.

One thing most griffins have in common is that they are very large. Most of them have the head and wings of a bird, the body of a lion, and a snake tail.

The griffin originally came from India, or so the stories say, where they made huge nests from gold that they found in the mountains. Griffins have the keen sight of eagles and the strength and courage of lions. This may explain why Byron, the *Spiderwick* griffin, is such a hero in the end when he fights off a dragon at the trash dump ogre lair.

The last creature we'll talk about is the **unicorn.** In *Spiderwick,* when the fairies are telling the Grace children that humans have taken over the forests and threaten the fairies, a unicorn steps over to Mallory and rubs her with its horn. This unicorn is white with a long mane.

Traditionally, a unicorn is a large horse with one horn in the middle of its forehead. Mallory's unicorn is the size of a deer; otherwise, it is the same as the traditional unicorn.

Some legends tell of unicorns that have goat beards, antelope legs, and lion tails. Some scholars believe that people thought they were seeing unicorns, when in actuality they were really seeing rhinoceroses. I find it hard to believe that anyone would mistake a rhinoceros for a unicorn. One is gigantic, fat, and gray, with a huge head: the rhino. The other is the size of a deer or horse, slender, and white, with a delicate head: the unicorn. The only thing they have in common is the fact that they both have horns.

In 400 B.C., a Greek doctor named Ctesias wrote that he'd seen a unicorn that looked like an Indian horse with a white body, a purple head, and a single horn. In fact, unicorns have been mentioned by many famous, ancient writers, including Aristotle. The key factor about the traditional unicorn that relates it directly to the *Spiderwick* unicorn is that when these unicorns touch a person with their horns, the person is healed in some way, protected from harm, and endowed with special qualities and abilities. Just like the *Spiderwick* unicorn, the traditional unicorn is sweet and docile, and will come up to strangers and gently touch them.

I'd like to believe in fairies, brownies, and unicorns. It could be argued that there's no proof that these creatures exist. But on the other hand, there's also no proof that they *don't* exist.

Fast Fact Quiz!

Where does time flow at a different pace from time in the real world?

○ Answer 1: Other planets throughout the universe.

○ Answer 2: The Land of ogres and trolls.

○ Answer 3: Fairyland.

○ Answer 4: All of the above.

✦ 6 ✦
Which Magical Being
Are *You?*

In this chapter, you can match a bunch of your
personal attributes with those of various magical
creatures. Then you can try and figure out
which magical being you would be, if indeed you
could be one.

Here's how you play the game. Answer each
question as truthfully as you can. After you finish, I'll tell you how to add up your score. You'll
get a certain number of points for each answer.
After you add up your score, check your results.
Based on your total score, I'll tell you which

magical creature is the most similar in personality to *you*. I'll take this little quiz myself, so I'll let you know what my score indicates: am I like a goblin, an ogre, a troll? I hope not. I'd rather have my game results tell me that I'm most like a pixie or light elf, but I won't know until I take the quiz.

Sharpen your pencils (or your gum wads, if you're going to stick gum on the page to mark your answers). And here we go . . .

1. Do you get in a lot of trouble with your parents and teachers?

$\bigcirc$ Yes $\bigcirc$ No

2. When you get in trouble, are you usually being blamed for stuff you didn't even do?

$\bigcirc$ Yes $\bigcirc$ No

3. Do you live in the walls of your kitchen?

$\bigcirc$ Yes $\bigcirc$ No

4. Do you like to play pranks and practical jokes on people?

      ○ Yes   ○ No

5. Do you dream about throwing eggs around the house or smearing catsup on the walls?

      ○ Yes   ○ No

6. Are tigers your favorite food?

      ○ Yes   ○ No

7. Are you really considerate of other people's feelings?

      ○ Yes   ○ No

8. If you see a stranger who is hurt, do you feel compelled (that means "forced") to help him?

      ○ Yes   ○ No

9. If you see a stranger who is hurt, do you shriek with laughter and call him a loser-jerk?

      ○ Yes   ○ No

10. If you see a bird with a broken wing on the ground, do you tell someone, like your mother?

    ○ Yes   ○ No

11. If you see a bird with a broken wing on the ground, do you stomp on it and cackle like a witch?

    ○ Yes   ○ No

12. If you were lost in the Amazon jungle, would you slap a monkey around?

    ○ Yes   ○ No

13. Does your breath melt ice?

    ○ Yes   ○ No

14. Do people complain that your breath is burning holes in their flesh?

    ○ Yes   ○ No

15. Are your fingernails black with filth?

    ○ Yes   ○ No

16. Do you believe in Santa Claus?

        ◯ Yes ◯ No

17. Do you like to go to lots of parties?

        ◯ Yes ◯ No

18. Do you like to play musical instruments?

        ◯ Yes ◯ No

19. Do you like to create paintings and drawings?

        ◯ Yes ◯ No

20. Are you a calm, patient person?

        ◯ Yes ◯ No

21. Are you usually hysterical and shrieking like a mad man (or, if you're a girl, like a crazy lady)?

        ◯ Yes ◯ No

22. Have you ever seen the belly-button fairy?

        ◯ Yes ◯ No

23. At your birthday party, do you serve friends crumbs rather than entire pieces of cake?

⭕ Yes ⭕ No

24. Are you invisible to most people?

⭕ Yes ⭕ No

25. Are you over ten feet tall?

⭕ Yes ⭕ No

26. When standing, are you as tall as your friend's knee?

⭕ Yes ⭕ No

27. Have you ever wanted to spend your life guarding jewels and other treasures?

⭕ Yes ⭕ No

28. Have you ever wanted to spend your life guarding a trash dump?

⭕ Yes ⭕ No

29. Do you snarl "Roast the pigs!" more than once a day?

    ○ Yes   ○ No

30. If you were a horse, would you live on land?

    ○ Yes   ○ No

31. If you were a horse, would you live in the water?

    ○ Yes   ○ No

32. If you come across objects (such as seeds) that are scattered everywhere or are terribly disorganized, do you feel compelled to organize and count them?

    ○ Yes   ○ No

33. Would you like to spend all day every day for the rest of your life wailing under the windows of people who are about to die?

    ○ Yes   ○ No

34. Would you like to spend all day twice a week wailing under the windows of people who are about to die?

    ○ Yes ○ No

35. Are you interested in fixing shoes?

    ○ Yes ○ No

36. Is it easy to trick you and play pranks on you?

    ○ Yes ○ No

37. Are you sweet and gentle?

    ○ Yes ○ No

38. Do you dream about having sleepovers and playing games underneath bridges?

    ○ Yes ○ No

39. Are you courageous and loyal, like the lion in *The Wizard of Oz*?

    ○ Yes ○ No

40. Do you collect your friends' teeth and save them in a special treasure box?

    ⭘ Yes ⭘ No

Did you check Yes or No for every question? Make sure you answer them all, or you could end up being a troll when you're really a household brownie.

Scoring!

Step 1.

For each Yes you answered for the following questions, give yourself 10 points (for example, if you answered Yes for question 1, write "10" next to question 1; if you also answered Yes for question 5, write "10" next to question 5): Questions 1, 4, 5, 6, 9, 11, 12, 15, 21, 25, 29, 32, 36, 38.

For each Yes you answered for the following questions, give yourself 5 points: Questions 13, 14, 27, 28, 31, 33, 34, 35.

For each Yes you answered for the following questions, give yourself 1 point: Questions 2, 3, 26.

For every remaining Yes you answered for a question, give yourself 0 points. (For example, if you answered Yes for question 7, write "0" next to question 7.)

Step 2.

Add up your scores. Write your grand total here: _____

My score happens to be 10 + 10 + 5 = 25

I have a very low score. What does this mean? Well, sum up your score and write it down, and read on!

Step 3.

If your score is between 0 and 50, this means you are a nice magical creature. You might be a household brownie, a light elf, a fun-loving sprite, a griffin, a unicorn, or even a tooth fairy.

If your score is between 51 and 75, you're probably the type of magical creature who likes to play pranks on people. Possibly, you're a woeful (sad) form of fairy, but you don't actually cause trouble to anybody. Possibly you just have smelly, hot breath. You might be a leprechaun, a banshee, a phooka, or a dragon.

If you score exceeds 75 (that is, if your score is higher than 75), you're a dangerous kind of magical creature. You might be a boggart, a goblin, a troll, or a fairy of the Unseelie Court.

Specifics!

If you really want to know what type of magical creature you resemble, here's a good way to tell:

If you answered Yes to question 1, you're probably similar to a boggart, troll, goblin, or leprechaun.

If you answered Yes to questions 2 and 3, you're an awful lot like a household brownie.

If you answered Yes to questions 4 and 5, you resemble a boggart or leprechaun.

Clearly, a Yes to question 6 means you're a goblin.

And if you also answered Yes to questions 9, 11, 29, and 32, you're definitely a goblin.

A Yes to question 12 means you're a fairy of the Unseelie Court.

If you answered Yes to questions 13 and 14, you're a dragon.

If you answered Yes to questions 15, 25, 36, and 38, you could be a troll.

If you answered Yes to questions 33 and 34, you might be a banshee.

A Yes to question 35 clearly indicates you're a borderline leprechaun.

If you answered Yes to questions 17, 18, 19, and 20, you might be a light elf.

If you answered Yes to questions 7, 8, 10, 23, and 35, you might be a sprite or a unicorn. It's also possible you're a griffin, particularly if you answered Yes to question 39.

With my score of 25, I'm a type of nice magical creature. I might be a household brownie, a light elf, a fun-loving sprite, a griffin, a unicorn, or even a tooth fairy. I did answer Yes to questions 1 and 2, indicating that I might be a household brownie or a boggart. I also answered Yes to question 31, meaning I could be a phooka. I'd rather think that I am indeed most like a sprite. I wonder what kind of magical creature you turned out to be. I'd also like to think that there are some unicorns out there, as well as some light elves and tooth fairies.

Fast Fact Quiz!

Griffins are:

○ Answer 1: an exotic form of breakfast doughnut.

○ Answer 2: french fries shaped like lion-birds.

○ Answer 3: giant magical birds with the sight of eagles and the courage of lions.

○ Answer 4: white horses with single horns on their foreheads.

A Story About a Japanese Mermaid

From the waist up, mermaids are beautiful girls. From the waist down, they are fish. In Japan, they are known as *ningyo,* and they're a lot like the mermaids in English stories. In 1989, the Walt Disney Company released a very popular movie called *The Little Mermaid.* You've probably seen this movie. It was loosely based on an 1836 poem, "The Little Mermaid," by the Danish poet Hans Christian Andersen.

In the poem, a mermaid falls in love with a prince from the land, who comes to the edge of the water to look for her. The only way the mermaid can be with the prince is if she has legs and can walk upon the land. So she gives a witch her tongue, and in return, the witch gives legs to the mermaid. While she finds love with her prince, she is in terrible pain walking on the legs, which feel like swords.

In addition to Disney's *The Little Mermaid,* other movies have been made about Hans Christian Andersen's mermaid. For example, in 1985, the movie *Splash* featured Darryl Hannah in the role of the mermaid and Tom Hanks in the role of the "prince."

The Japanese *ningyo*, or mermaid, is a water-dwelling fairy, and like many fairy spirits, she can be beautiful and helpful, or she can be conniving and deadly. The Japanese mermaid wears a long, flowing silk gown, even while swimming underwater. Her home is a palace with beautiful gardens at the bottom of the ocean.

The *ningyo* offers human men endless spiritual

and physical bliss, but of course there are dangers involved with such temptation. As with other realms of Fairyland, a human who lives with a *ningyo* has no sense of mortal time. If he eats mermaid food, it's as if he's eaten the fairy fruits of *Spiderwick*. He will no longer eat normal human food.

The folktale about Urashima Taro, a Japanese fisherman, and a mermaid is famous. In this story, Urashima sees some boys torturing a turtle, and the old fisherman saves the turtle's life. The turtle ends up being his companion, and Urashima kindly lets the creature loose to return to the ocean.

The next day, Urashima is in his fishing boat, dreaming about being a turtle himself. He hears someone calling his name, and lo and behold, it's the turtle, who thanks Urashima for saving his life.

The turtle brings Urashima to the palace of the underwater Dragon King of the Sea. The palace is beautiful and crafted of coral and mother-of-pearl. Beautiful fish bring Urashima and the turtle to visit with a sea princess, or *ningyo* mermaid.

Naturally, Urashima lives in total bliss with the mermaid for many days. He's madly in love and cannot tear himself away from the sea princess or her palace garden. But then he remembers that his elderly parents are still living on the land, and he tells the mermaid that he must return to the land and tell his parents about his new life. He doesn't want his parents to worry about him.

The mermaid tries to persuade him to stay with her beneath the sea, but when he insists that he must see his parents, she sighs, gives in to his wishes, and provides him with a beautiful box as a parting gift. She tells him never to open the box.

Urashima returns to the land, riding on the turtle's back. When he goes to his old village, he finds that while it looks pretty much the same, everyone living there is new to him. Even the houses look slightly different.

With everyone a stranger, it's hard for Urashima to find his parents. Nobody knows who they are! Finally, someone tells Urashima that a man with his name, Urashima Taro, lived in the village more than three hundred years ago. Of course, Urashima is shocked because he thinks he's only been gone for a few days. Remember, he was in Fairyland, where time stretches in very bizarre ways.

Of course, Urashima cannot see his parents, because they died more than three hundred years ago. Very sad, Urashima goes to the edge of the water again, where he sits in the sand and opens the mermaid's box. He opens it out of simple curiosity, nothing more. He can't resist seeing what's inside.

Big mistake!

As soon as he opens the box, his skin begins to

wrinkle, and suddenly he feels extremely old. Within seconds, he is dead of old age. After all, outside of Fairyland, Urashima is hundreds of years old.

The mermaid had given him bliss for a few days, but she'd also given him the curse of Fairyland, where time stretches longer than human time.

✦ 7 ✦
Top Ten List

This is *my* top ten list of favorite things that happen in *The Spiderwick Chronicles*. You may have a different list of top ten favorite things. For example, I wasn't too thrilled when the goblins were roasting animals. I did think it was pretty cool that there were cages lined with poison ivy and housing skeletons and barely alive creatures.

You can start each one by thinking to yourself: I like it when . . .

○ Number 10: Mallory wakes up and finds her hair is tied to the bedposts. When I was Mallory's age, I had hair that hung to my waist, and it was always in knots. I tied it in ponytails and secured it to the top of my head using big clips. At night, to keep the hair from knotting, I'd ball it into a big knot at the bottom of my head, then try really hard not to turn over in my sleep. As you might imagine, this was hard to do . . . while sleeping. The thought of having all that hair tied to the bedposts is horrifying.

○ Number 9: Jared scatters flour on the floor to attract the boggart. The next morning, the kitchen has been destroyed, and Jared's mother assumes he came downstairs in the middle of the night and went nuts, flinging eggs everywhere and squirting chocolate syrup on the walls. I like this part because it's funny, simple as that. I don't think my mother would have believed me had I blamed household disasters on boggarts. And she would have been furious had I sprinkled flour on the floor.

○ Number 8: Mallory uses her rapier (fencing sword) to fight off goblins, who are dragging Jared across the yard. Again, I like this part because it's funny. It almost sounds like fun to battle goblins with a rapier; as long as you win, that is.

○ Number 7: Simon decides that the children must save Byron, the griffin, and they drag the giant bird home on a tarp. They keep him in the dilapidated carriage house and nurse him back to health. Somehow, their mother doesn't know that a griffin is living in the carriage house. I haven't a clue how their mother doesn't notice that a huge prehistoric-like fairy bird thing is living in a ramshackle structure by the house. Doesn't she hear the thing cawing at night? Or maybe griffins don't caw. But then, doesn't she notice all the feathers?

○ Number 6: Mallory wonders how she and her brothers can possibly fight off an army of goblins, a dragon, and a shape-shifting ogre. The key is to get advice from Arthur Spiderwick, and to do that, the children have to convince the elves to give them access to Arthur. This part is fun because the elves are interesting. They're worried about the future of all elves, they're worried about the forest, and they're delicate yet strong creatures.

○ Number 5: Jared defends himself against the "Not-Jared," who is really Mulgarath the Ogre, pretending to be Jared. When a squabble breaks out between the real Jared and the Not-Jared, a vice principal shows up and blames everything on the real Jared. Then a fairy turns into a "Not-Mallory" and runs into the girl's bathroom. And then, to top off all these bad events, Mallory disappears, just as Simon had disappeared earlier. This part reminds me of the

Bizarros in *Superman* comics. The Bizarros were "Not-Supermans."

○ Number 4: Jared, Simon, and Mallory visit Aunt Lucinda, and sprites fly into her hospital room and fly around her head. They offer fairy fruits to the children. Apparently, the fairy fruits are so good that Aunt Lucinda has eaten nothing else since she ate her first fairy fruit long ago. I like the ideas of sprites and fairy fruits. I've been interested in fairies for a long time, and sprites are tiny, very delicate fairies. They sound innocent and beautiful. The thought that sprites are dancing around an old age home, dishing out fairy fruits to the elderly Aunt Lucinda is amusing.

○ Number 3: Jared wears the strange nose-clipped eyepiece for the first time. It's a very cool idea that someone can wear a special eyepiece that lets him see fairies and other magical creatures. It's much less appealing to think that a goblin can spit in your eyes to give you the same ability.

○ Number 2: Jared sees Thimbletack for the first time in the secret library room. After Jared, Simon, and Mallory leave a note for Thimbletack, apologizing for intruding into the boggart's house, they return to the secret room to find Thimbletack waiting for them. He stands about as tall as a pencil and has Simon's pet mice on leashes. I gasped and laughed when they saw Thimbletack for the first time. I was waiting for a fairy to enter the book, and there he was! Then I couldn't wait for him to talk and do things. And of course, he didn't let me down at all.

○ Number 1: My favorite part of *The Spiderwick Chronicles* has to be the illustrations. I thought for a long time about what to choose as my Number 1 favorite thing about the *Spiderwick* books. There's no question that I loved all the pictures drawn by Tony DiTerlizzi. Without the pictures, I wouldn't have liked the books nearly as much as I did—not to say that the story wasn't great, too, of course! But I stared at each picture for a long time.

Fast Fact Quiz!

The best way to beat a dwarf is to:

○ Answer 1: feed him noodles and cabbage.

○ Answer 2: shove him into the sunlight so he'll turn to stone right away.

○ Answer 3: put him in a locked cage lined with poison ivy and make sure the key is nearby.

○ Answer 4: make him wear an orange dunce cap.

✦ Appendix A ✦
Glossary

Bioluminescence. According to Simon, bioluminescence is a bluish glow from the fungi in the quarry. He's right. Bioluminescence is indeed a light that is caused by a chemical reaction inside a living entity. It's not the same as fluorescence, in which energy from a light source is absorbed by something and then emitted again. It's as if the light is sucked in, then shoved back out. In bioluminescence, the energy comes from a chemical reaction instead of an existing light source.

Boggart (Fairy). According to The Field Guide, a boggart is a brownie who goes nuts and starts doing really bad things. In real life fairy lore, boggarts are ill-tempered, mean, ugly-as-sin brownies. They completely destroy everything they don't like. They are shape-shifters, taking many different forms. Boggarts in human form are far more dangerous than boggarts who appear in other forms. Boggarts play tricks, and they also scare and hurt people.

Brownie (Fairy). According to The Field Guide, a brownie is a tiny man who lives in someone's house. In real fairy lore, a house brownie is a shaggy, very short man. He wears a ragged suit and small cap. The brownie does indeed adopt a house, and he emerges at night to do chores or cause problems. Brownies, according to real-life tradition, do indeed like bowls of milk, just like Thimbletack in *Spiderwick*. It is said that brownies are easily offended by what humans do. For example, if a person leaves too much milk in a bowl for the household brownie, the brownie may get really upset and leave the house forever.

Calamity. This is a disaster, a big mess. It is an event that causes loss and lasting distress. For example, Jared's mother always blames him for the calamities, or big messy disasters, that happen in their house, in Aunt Lucinda's hospital room, and at Mallory's fencing match.

Deflect. To deflect something means to avoid it or push it away, such as when Simon uses a parry to deflect Mallory's sword.

Dilapidated. Broken down and in ruins, such as the carriage house in the Grace's yard. In fact, their entire house is somewhat dilapidated.

Dragon. A dragon is a monster that looks like a huge reptile with lion's claws, a snake tail, and sometimes wings. In *Spiderwick*, the dragon is what is commonly referred to as a wyrm dragon (well, it's commonly referred to as a wyrm dragon by people who actually spend lots of time thinking about dragons). A wyrm dragon has no wings, and his red scaled body is snake-like. His head looks like a cross between a dragon's head and a horse's head. Sometimes, he has horns. He *always* has fangs. He breathes fire and is pure evil. He lives in smelly, stinking, rotting places such as swamps and trash dumps.

Dumbwaiter. A dumbwaiter is a bucket-type device that hauls Jared up and down between the floors of the house. In olden days, in real life, it was used to transport food, dishes, and other things from the kitchen to the upstairs rooms.

Dwarf. Dwarves are small and look like mis-shapen humans. They usually have long, gray beards and look really old. They are also miners, according to legend, so their role in *Spiderwick* conforms to what we know about dwarves. Rumors say that dwarves are toads during the day. If the dwarves are hit by sunlight, they turn to stone. According to folklore, dwarves turn metal into beautiful but dangerous artifacts. These artifacts possess spells and curses.

Elf. Light Elves live high in the sky and are compassionate and kind. Dark Elves, on the other hand, live beneath the ground and are nasty creatures. According to standard fairy lore, elves are pretty tall compared to most fairies, who are so small we can barely see them. Elves stand from 4'10" to 5'8" or more. They're slim and delicate, with huge eyes of beautiful colors. The *Spiderwick* elves are probably Light Elves rather than Dark Elves.

Fairy. Fairies are tiny, imaginary creatures who look like humans and who possess magical powers. They're often clever and mischievous. As depicted in books and paintings, fairies are usually called *good people,* even though they're also thought to be somewhat unruly and hard to control. In real life, as in *The Spiderwick Chronicles,* fairies are considered to be shape-shifters by those who believe in them. Fairies supposedly live in mounds (small hills). Time flows at a different pace in Fairyland than in our world. If you spend an hour in Fairyland and then return to our world, you suddenly might be ten years older.

Fencing. This is the sport of using a foil, épée, or saber in attack and defense maneuvers. Fencers in modern times practice and compete on strips that are called *pistes.*

Foil. Mallory probably uses a foil when she fences. A foil is one of three main types of swords used by fencers. It has a flexible blade and weighs about one pound.

Fool's Gold. Similar in color to gold, this non-gold ore is often mistaken for the real thing. Fool's gold is likely to be iron pyrite or muscovite (white mica).

Goblin. When Jared first sees goblins through his nose-clipped eyepiece, he thinks that they have faces like frogs and dead-white eyes. He describes them as green with bloated, hairless bodies, and with teeth that look like jagged glass and rocks. In real folklore, goblins are nasty little creatures who dwell in fairyland. They're ugly as sin, they steal anything they can get their claws on, and they like to lure people to certain death by dangling fairy fruits and other items in front of them. When standing, the top of a goblin's head might reach your knee. He usually doesn't look like a frog, as in *Spiderwick,* but rather he appears as an old man with a long, gray beard. Goblins generally like children and give them presents and treats, but the goblins dislike adults and tend to disrupt households by wrecking kitchens and furniture.

Griffin. These are huge mythical birds. Some stories say that griffins are part bird and part lion; others describe griffins that are mostly lions with eagles' heads. When a griffin is mostly lion, it often doesn't even have wings. One thing most griffins have in common is that they are very large. Most of them have the head and wings of a bird, the body of a lion, and a snake tail. The griffin originally came from India, or so the stories say, where they made huge nests from gold that they found in the mountains. Griffins have the keen sight of eagles and the strength and courage of lions. This may explain why Byron, the *Spiderwick* griffin, is such a hero in the end when he fights off a dragon at the trash dump ogre lair.

Hobgoblin. Hobgoblins are closely related to brownies. They are usually drawn by artists as looking like ugly, little elves. They help humans do household chores, just like their brownie cousins. Although hobgoblins share the "goblins" part of their names with the evil goblins, the two are quite different: hobgoblins are good-natured and kind, though easily offended by what humans do.

Jewelweed. As Jared and Mallory look for Simon, they go through the woods, stepping in jewelweed. This is the common name for a plant called *Balsaminaceae.* The common name is much easier to remember and pronounce. Jewelweed are actually beautiful flowers that look like impatiens, which are commonly grown in summer gardens. Some forms of jewelweed, however, can be as tall as five feet and look like bushes. The spotted jewelweed, for example, grows in dense clusters with many five-foot-tall bushes packed tightly together. It would be hard to make it through a forest filled with vines and jewelweed, but this is what Jared and Mallory do.

Leprechaun (Fairy). Leprechauns make and mend shoes. If your shoe needs a new sole, a leprechaun could sneak into your closet, grab the shoe while you're asleep, put a new sole on it, and then return it before you wake up. Actually, the leprechaun's original name was *luchorpan,* which means "little body." A long time ago, a luchorpan was also thought to be a dwarf. The typical leprechaun is constantly hammering away at shoes, so if you hear constant tapping in your walls, you may have a leprechaun in the house. He guards crocks of gold, too, and he plays pranks on humans all the time.

Nixie (Fairy). Jared wonders if nixies are in the stream by the house. Nixies are water spirits, found primarily in folklore in Scandinavia,

Switzerland, and Germany. They're beautiful, female, and have fishtails. While mermaids live in oceans, nixies live in fresh water streams.

Obstinate. This word is used to refer to someone who is being very stubborn.

Ogre. These are giants born from a merging of Orcus, the Roman god of death and darkness, and Saturn, a god who supposedly ate Hungarian tribes for dessert. Ogres have ugly faces, lots of body hair, and they have big humps on their backs. They smell like garbage, which is probably why the *Spiderwick* ogre lives in a trash dump. Many ogres wear enchanted boots, which enable them to run quickly. Ogres are thieves and will steal anything.

Parry. In fencing, the word *parry* means that you're deflecting or avoiding a sword thrust. If

Joe thrusts his sword at me, I parry to the left, then I parry to the right, and maybe I duck—and most likely, I run—but that's beside the point.

Phooka. Jared describes phookas as looking like monkeys with speckled, black-brown fur and long tails. The *Spiderwick* phooka has long tufts of fur around its neck and a rabbit's face with rabbit ears and whiskers. Jared explains to Simon and Mallory that phookas are shape-shifters. It is true that phookas are sometimes considered Irish goblins who assume the shapes of various strange mythical creatures and beasts. According to some stories, phookas sport black fur, feathers, and skin. So Jared's phooka could indeed look like a monkey with speckled fur and a rabbit's head. According to most legends, however, phookas are monstrous water horses who haunt streams and lakes, trying to entice victims to mount them. If someone mounts a phooka, the beast bolts into the water or over a cliff, sending its rider to his death.

Pixie (Fairy). Jared wonders if pixies are in the yard. In real folklore, pixies are tiny fairies who travel in packs. They usually have red hair, young faces, and pointed ears. If you give pixies new clothes, they will feel compelled to leave your house and never return.

Quarry. This is a huge pit containing stones and gravel.

Rambunctious. Unruly and hard to control, full of energy. Thimbletack is rambunctious and throws eggs around the kitchen.

Rapier. This is a long sword with no cutting edge. It has only a point and is used for thrusting during fencing matches. Long ago, a rapier was a two-edged sword used mainly in the sixteenth and seventeenth centuries.

Riposte. This refers to a quick sword thrust after you parry someone else's fencing attack.

Shape-shifter. This refers to the ability to transform your physical appearance into another, totally different form. An example of shape-shifting might be when a fairy who looks like a girl turns herself into a cat, tree, or harp.

Sprite (Fairy). A sprite is mischievous and unpredictable. He's tiny and elusive, which means he's hard to catch.

Troll. In reality, a troll is usually described as a hairy, old man with a long beard. Some trolls are huge and evil. Some sport humps on their backs and have gigantic noses. In the woods,

Jared and Mallory are looking for Simon, when they come to a stream and Mallory falls into the water. Out of the water rises a troll, and Jared describes him as having a head that's the color of rotting green grass, small black eyes, a gnarled nose, cracked teeth, and extremely long fingers.

Unicorn. In *Spiderwick,* when the fairies are telling the Grace children that humans have taken over the forests and threatened the fairies, a unicorn steps over to Mallory and rubs her with its horn. This unicorn is white with a long mane. Traditionally, a unicorn is a large horse with one horn in the middle of its forehead. Mallory's unicorn is the size of a deer; otherwise, it is the same as the traditional unicorn.

✦ Appendix B ✦
Cheat Sheet

Answers to Fast Fact Quizzes

1. So What's It All About?

Marc is:

☑ Answer 3: the editor of this book.

2. Are You a *Spiderwick* Fanatic?

A boggart is:

☑ Answer 3: a naughty brownie.

3. *Spiderwick* Characters: Good Guys vs. Scum and Filth

An ogre is:

☑ Answer 2: a huge monster with a horned head.

4. Who Are *Your* Favorite Characters?

A dumbwaiter is:

✓ Answer 2: a basket-like device that moves between floors in a house.

5. Magical Beings

Where does time flow at a different pace from time in the real world?

✓ Answer 4: All of the above.

6. Which Magical Being Are *You?*

Griffins are:

✓ Answer 3: giant magical birds with the sight of eagles and the courage of lions.

7. Top Ten List

The best way to beat a dwarf is to:

✓ Answer 2: shove him into the sunlight so he'll turn to stone right away.